YO U R

LI F E

HOW TO SURVIVE THE REST OF YOUR LIFE

YOUR LIFE

SURVIVAL KIT INSTRUCTIONS

There are four main sections to help get you
through the rest of your life in good nick.

EVERYDAY CHALLENGES are the simple, daily
chances we have to let the living word of God
transform our minds and attitudes.

MAKING CONNECTIONS is about our thoughts and
feelings: bringing them to God and being open
to others. None of us can make it on our own.

IN A NUTSHELL takes up the main elements of
our faith — THE most valuable part of any
survival kit.

THOUGHTS AND MEMORIES are a record of friends
and events important to treasure for life.

Enjoy!

survive

ow to survive the rest of your life

Pauline
BOOKS & MEDIA
www.pauline-uk.org

a practical user's guide

HOW TO SURVIVE THE REST OF YOUR LIFE
First published in Great Britain 2006
Pauline Books & Media
Middle Green, Slough SL3 6BS
www.pauline-uk.org

EVERYDAY CHALLENGES, MAKING CONNECTIONS, THOUGHTS AND MEMORIES
written by Dermott Donnelly

IN A NUTSHELL
written by Gerard Conroy

Scripture quotations are taken from
The Christian Community Bible
© Bernardo Hurault 1999

Graphic design and photographs by Pauline Books & Media, Middle Green, Slough
except the following photographs:
Alves – 28, 29, 48, 49, 54, 55, 83   Ballini – 40, 41, 44, 76, 77

ISBN 190478505

Printed in the EEC by AGAM, Cuneo, Italy
www.agam.it

CONTENTS

>>> everyday challenges

As we go through life
each day presents us
with challenges
that will shape us
according to the way we manage them.

The living Word of God
gives us light
for every situation in our life.

This Word is an essential part
of our survival kit.

It is the Word
we can utterly count on
as true and a rock
on which to build our lives,
securely.

EVERYDAY
CHALLENGES

As we go through life
each day presents
with challenges
that will
according to

The Living Word of
gives us light
for every situation in o

This Word is an essential
of our survival kit.

It is the Word
we can utterly count on
as true and a rock.
which to build our lives
securely

CHALLENGES

Life is not about how much we earn but how much we love.

Don't let yourselves be shaped
by the world where you live, but rather
be transformed through the renewal of your mind.
You must discern the will of God:
what is good, what pleases, what is perfect.
Romans 12:2

Life

is the greatest gift we have been given ---
live it to the full!

Life

I have come
that they may have life,
life in all its fullness.
John 10:10

Holding a grudge
   is like
carrying a heavy weight inside
   that affects
every relationship in life.

Peter asked Jesus,
"Lord, how many times
must I forgive the offence
of my brother or sister?
Seven times?"
Jesus answered him,
"No, not seven times but
seventy-seven times."
cf Matthew 18:21

Forgiving someone
who has hurt us
is not about letting them off
>>>>>>>>> but letting ourselves be free.

forgiving

forgiving

forgiving

forgiving

Jesus said,
"Father, forgive them >>>>>>>>>
for they do not know what they do".
Luke 23:34

Listening

talking talking talking talking talking talking...

Happy are
those who
hear
the Word of God
and **do it.**

Listening twice as much as talking
helps us
grow in
>>>>>>>>>> wisdom.

Let the wise listen
and they will learn yet more.>>>>>>>>>
cf Proverbs 1:5

No one can ever take away the reality that
each of us
is a unique creation.

uniQue creAtion

creAtioN

creAtion

creAtioN

creAtioN

creAtion

It is in Christ
that we were
claimed
as God's own,
chosen from
the beginning.
cf Ephesians 1:11

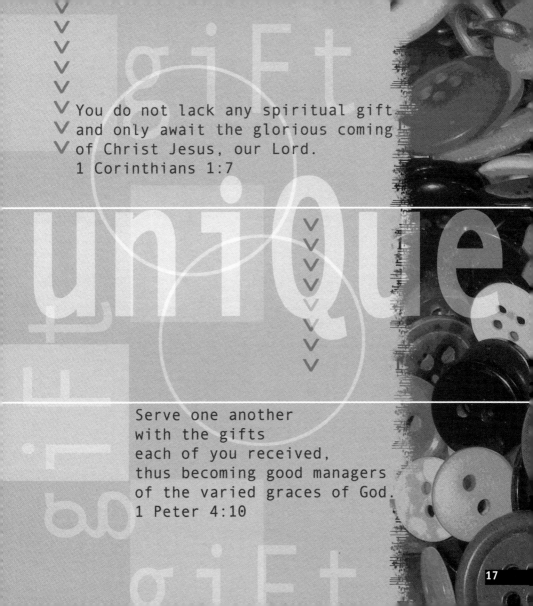

You do not lack any spiritual gift
and only await the glorious coming
of Christ Jesus, our Lord.
1 Corinthians 1:7

Serve one another
with the gifts
each of you received,
thus becoming good managers
of the varied graces of God.
1 Peter 4:10

but look
to the future
with hope...

Don't look back with anger in your heart

Forgetting what is behind me,
I race forward and run
towards the goal...
to which God has called us.
Philippians 3:13-14

hope

never
underestimate
the power
of
prayer.

The Lord is
near those
who call on him,
who call
trustfully
upon his name.
Psalm 145:18

nothing is

FREE

someone
must
always pay
the price.

See how God showed
his love for us:
while we were
still sinners,
Christ died for us.
Romans 5:8

Look **beyond** what seems achievable >>>>>>>>>>>> to what **you** are called to achieve.

∨
∨
∨
∨
∨

If you wish to be
> > > > > > > perfect come and follow me.
Matthew 19:21

Let loyalty and kindness
never leave you:
tie them around your neck,
write them on the tablet of your heart.
Proverbs 3:3

finding true love
makes us whole...

...and true love
always brings **freedom.**

friend

True friendship is
most priceless...........

V
V
V
V
V
V
V
V
V
V
V
V

Some friends
only bring ruin,

others are
closer than a brother or a sister.
Proverbs 18:24

The best thing you can give to another is yourself.

Just as I have loved you,
you also must love one another.
John 13:34

give

receive

Always
give generously
and receive all gifts
with true gratitude.

Each of you should give as you decided personally,
and not reluctantly as if obliged.
God *loves* a cheerful giver.
2 Corinthians 9:7

May Christ
dwell in
your hearts
through faith;
may you
be rooted
and founded
in love...

That you
may know the
love of Christ
which surpasses
all knowledge,
that you may be
filled
and reach the
fullness of God.
Ephesians 3:17,19

ultimate
love

prayer

allows us

to communicate

with

ultimate

Love.

Don't settle for what is on the surface

look beyond it
to discover
the **treasure**...

For where your treasure is,
there also your heart will be.
Matthew 6:21

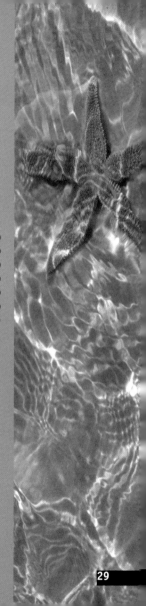

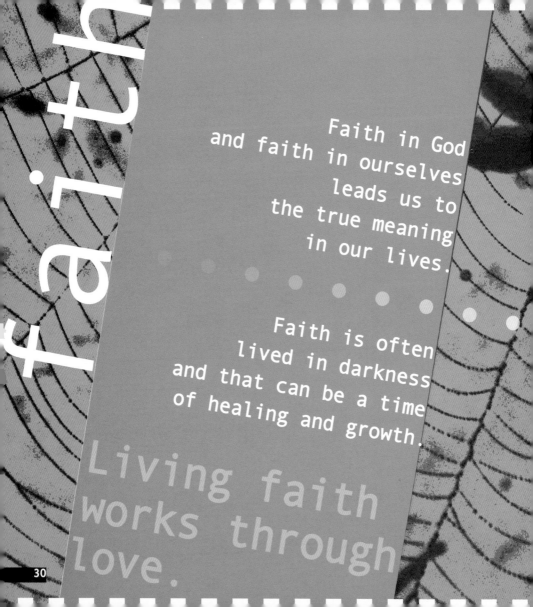

faith

Faith in God
and faith in ourselves
leads us to
the true meaning
in our lives.

Faith is often
lived in darkness
and that can be a time
of healing and growth.

Living faith
works through
love.

At present
we see dimly
as in
a faulty mirror,
but then it shall be
face to face.
Now we know in part,
but then
I will know
as I am known.
1 Corinthians 13:12

faith

31

Wisdom
in life
isn't knowing
the conclusion
but the next
step that will
get us there.

You will show me
the path of life,
in your presence
the fullness of joy,
at your right hand
happiness forever.
Psalm 16:11

By this
everyone will know
that you are
my disciples,
if you have
love
for one another.
John 13:35

Above all,
let your love
for one another be sincere,
for love covers
a multitude of sins.
1 Peter 4:8

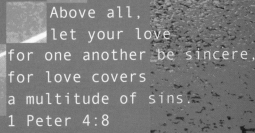

When we are on our own,
when we have shut our door at night,
when there is no one else around,
no one to impress,
Who am I?
What are my joys,
hopes,
fears,
insecurities
and dreams?

Whatever they are,
God is interested and he cares.

Prayer is our communication with God
and it is vital for our survival
as we go through life.

Speak to him from the heart.
He cares.
He will listen.

making conr

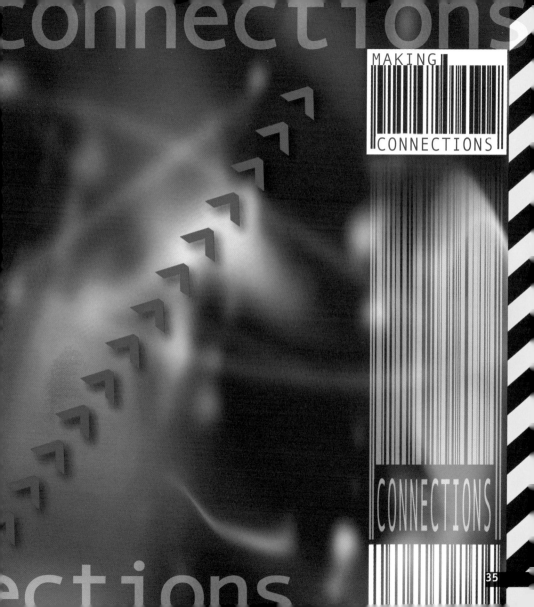

connections

CONNECTIONS

CONNECTIONS

ections

Our Father,

who art in heaven,
hallowed be thy name;
thy kingdom come;
thy will be done on earth
as it is in heaven.

Give us this day
our daily bread;
and forgive us our trespasses
as we forgive those
who trespass against us;
and lead us not
into temptation,
but deliver us
from evil.

Deliver us, Lord,
from every evil,
and grant us peace in our day.

In your mercy
keep us free from sin
and protect us
from all anxiety
as we wait
in joyful hope
for the coming of our Saviour,
Jesus Christ.

For the kingdom,
the power,
and the glory
are yours, now and forever.

Amen

Mary's Song

My soul proclaims the greatness of the Lord,
    my spirit exults in God my saviour!

He has looked upon his servant
        in her lowliness,
        and people forever will call me blessed.

The Mighty One has done great things for me,
        Holy is his name!

From age to age his mercy extends
        to those who live in his presence.
He has acted with power and done wonders
        and scattered the proud with their plans.

He has put down the mighty
        from their thrones and lifted up
        those who are downtrodden.

He has filled the hungry
        with good things
            but has sent the rich away empty.

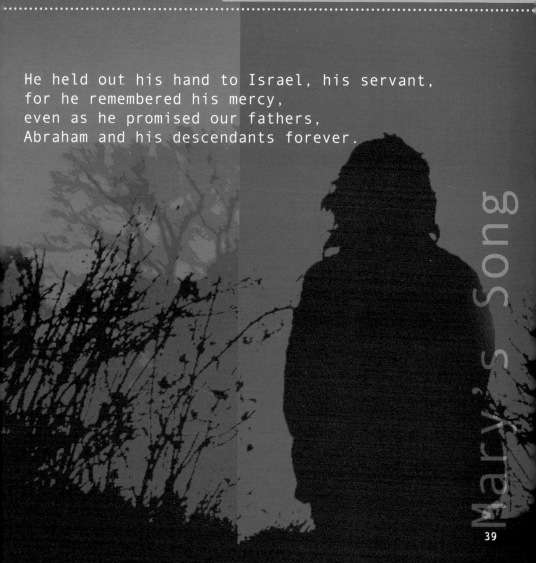

He held out his hand to Israel, his servant,
for he remembered his mercy,
even as he promised our fathers,
Abraham and his descendants forever.

Mary's Song

Father God,

As I approach the exam
that is ahead of me,
gift me with the skills
that I need in order to do my best.

I bring before you my nervousness
and my fears
along with my hopes
and my dreams
and invite you to be with me.

I pray that I experience
the calmness that the Spirit brings
and whatever the outcome
I will truly believe
in the unique person that I am.

Through Christ our Lord.

Amen

Lord God,

As I think about my future
and the decisions ahead
I pray for wisdom.

I pray
to make the right choices
     for me
          and those around me.

May I be always open
even if it is the hardest
decision to make.

Give me the strength
to accept all the implications
this will have
     on my future
          and bless me
as I journey through life.

Through Christ our Lord. Amen

← Cash machines
← Platforms 4 to 11
Platforms 2 and 3
Platform 1
King's Cross Thameslink
York Way Way out

for travelling

God our Father,

I invite you
to bless
the journey
that is ahead of me.

Be with me always
and keep me
free from all harm.

Through Christ
our Lord.

Amen

travelling

for travelling

Loving God,

I come before you
a unique and gifted individual.

However, I carry regrets
for the times I have failed.

In times of weakness
I have made the wrong decision
and often hurt others,
and so have not lived up to
my full potential.

I present to you those failures
whether actions, thoughts or words
and I ask for your forgiveness.

Bless me in the future
and through my life may I bring
hope, justice, love and joy
to the world in which I live.

Through Christ our Lord.

Amen

Lord,

You are the God of all peace.
I present to you
all places of conflict
in our world.

As there is no ideology,
political thought,
culture or particular
way of life
greater than
the life
of the humblest person,

I pray for peace.

In Jesus' name.

Amen

for peace

44

Lord,

I pray for all people
in our world
who do not have enough
to live on.

I think of all those
who do not have food,
clean water, medicines
and somewhere adequate to live.

I pray that I will always
be grateful for these things
which I take for granted each day
and may we
who have these resources in abundance
be willing to share our resources
with those who have not.

Through Christ our Lord. **Amen**

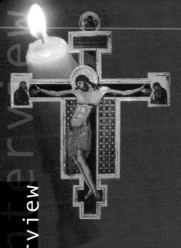

God of compassion,
Father of all life
I present to you my life,
   my joys,
         sorrows,
                     hopes
         and
               dreams.

As I place myself before this
interview panel,
I pray that you give me
the truth of believing in myself.
Help me know my gifts and limitations.
May I get this job
if it be right for me and if not,
help me to discern the future.
Let me never be dismayed
by the decision.
Give me a true confidence
and bless all I do at this time.

Amen

thanksgiving
for getting a job

Father God, I bless you
and praise you.
I thank you
for the gift
of this job.
Help me to grow
in respect
for my colleagues
and guide me
in the future.
I ask you this
through Christ,
our Lord.

Amen

thanksgiving
for getting a job

Lord,

There are times when I struggle to believe
especially when everything around me
does not speak of a God of love.

Help me discover you when it seems
impossible for you to be present.

Just as love is discovered
in the brutality of the Crucifixion,
help me discover faith
when darkness surrounds me.

May I walk in the light and be guided
    each step of the way
        by your loving presence in my life.

Amen

faith

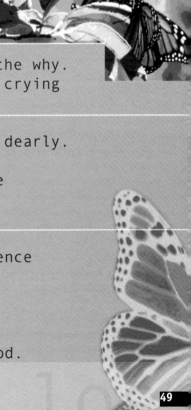

for the loss of a loved one

Father God,

You are the God of all life.

Help me, help me to understand the why.
My heart is hurting, my soul is crying
for meaning.

I have lost someone whom I love dearly.
How can life ever be the same
how can it ever be complete
how can my restless spirit
ever be calmed?

Help me, God, help me to experience
your presence.
Help me to feel the peace
that only you can give me.

Help me. Help me. Help me, my God.

Father,

God of Love,
Life offers me
many opportunities
and I am directed
towards a number of routes
which I can follow.

Help me on my journey
so that I can choose
each step wisely
and know the paths
that will lead to life.

Amen

for wisdom

God of love and friendship,

You created us
to share our lives with you
and each other.

I bring before you the difficulties
that I am facing in my relationships
at this time in my life.

Help me to look beyond my feelings
and so discover the feelings
of the other.

Help me to see this situation
in a new way
and with an openness
and a readiness to change.

Let any change that needs to take place
start with me.

Help me to know the next step
in order to bring your healing and peace
into this situation.

I pray this prayer
through Jesus my brother,
friend and Lord.

Amen

relationships

Lord of light,

I sometimes feel
I am living in the darkness,
without the desire
or the knowledge
of how to come to the light.

It is here that I place
my trust in you and ask you
to be the light for me.

When all around me is dark,
bathe me in your radiant light.

When the daily tasks
become mountains to climb,
be my strength.
When all my resources are done,
live,
breathe
and move in me
and help me discover once again
the adventure and the excitement
of the life that you gave me.

Amen

Father,

Open my eyes
    to see with a new sight,
open my heart
    to love in a new way,
open my ears
    that I may hear
    not only the cries of your people
    but your loving words of comfort.

Words that are sometimes whispered,
but life-giving words.
Words that bring
    life,
        light
            and love
into our everyday lives.

Amen

inspiration

Powerful God,

You created us
in your own likeness
and image.

Help me to grow more and more
in your presence.

I invite you
into the areas of my life where
there is a need for healing
and I ask you to make me whole.

May your powerful Spirit
move through my life
and bring healing and peace.

Through Christ our Lord.

Amen

healing

Lord,

Your word is a light that guides,
a power that heals
and a whisper that brings life.

As I ponder you powerful word
may I be guided by your Spirit
so that it may change
and transform me.

Help me to allow your word
to take flesh in me
that I may become
more like your son Jesus
who lives and reigns with you
and the Holy Spirit,
one God forever and ever.

Amen

your
word

IN A NUTSHELL

When we set out on a journey,
it can be fun to just take off
and see where we end up.

When we set out
on our journey through life,
we need similar times,
times for fun and the unexpected.

But we also need to have some security
and it helps if we can have
a few guidelines.

Faith gives us the security
and the guidelines that we need.

It is the part of our survival kit
that gives us a grounding
and enables us
to create something beautiful
in our life.

FAITH IN A

NUTSHELL

NUTSHELL

LIFE... TO THE FULL

I have come that you may have life and have it to the full. >>>>>>>>>>>>

cf John chapter ten verse ten

One of the most exciting things about growing up is realising just how much there is for us in life. 'I want it all and I want it now', just about sums it up. The joy of life and of what is beautiful and of what makes us feel good is all there for us – and we get to choose it! There is in all of us a desire to be filled with all of these things and to keep on being filled by them.

However, we can destroy ourselves by our desires. If we lose control of them, instead of blossoming, they

Do not let yourselves be shaped by the world where you live, but rather be transformed by your new mind. >>>>>>>>>>>>> cf Romans chapter twelve verse two

wither. If we refuse to compromise either our desires or the means of fulfilling them, we in fact compromise our freedom.

Or we can find a safer road through life; perhaps we don't try to become drunk with all that life has to offer. We can be more moderate in our appetites and negotiate our desires in order to live our life more fully.

The desire in us for life and for all that is beautiful was put in us by God. It is the dynamism in our life because it drives us on to search for something that will make us whole. But the mistake people often make in trying to fulfil their desires is that they don't go beyond the beauty they can see and hear and touch and smell and taste. They try to fill themselves up with things that can only satisfy their physical and emotional needs; they forget about their spiritual needs and thus they never find the completeness they long for; they stop at the beauty of creation and miss the even greater beauty of the creator.

When we feel the need to have space and time to find ourselves and to know ourselves better, that is when our spiritual desires are crying out for us to satisfy them.

our likeness"…male and female he created them

IMAGE AND LIKENESS

As we develop our personalities

we become our own
person, in search of
our own fulfilment,
distinct from that
of our parents. But
every so often, we do
things that remind
us of our parents.
When we have our
own children, as
they grow up, we
see in them little
mannerisms of our
parents. These remind
us of the unity that
runs through the
generations. Seeing

On that day yo

God said, "Let us make man in our image, to

this brings us a joy; it reminds us of where we have come from. And it gives us a joy that comes from knowing who we are.

In his life on earth, in his teaching and his actions, Christ frequently made reference to doing what he had seen his Father doing. He knew who he was and where he was from and this gave him strength for his life especially in the face of opposition.

We are made in the image and likeness of God and through our baptism we are formed in the image of Christ. This is who we are. It is something we can recognise in our actions and, like Christ, this gives us a solidity and strength for our life. It gives us the joy that comes from knowing where we belong.

Sin disrupts this image and confuses us, causing us to use our freedom in ways that we have not learned from God our Father, or his Son, Christ. It brings fear into our life, because it takes away that solidity and offers only shaky ground on which to build our life.

We find our true happiness, our fulfilment, our home when we recognise in our actions and mannerisms the things that remind us of Christ and the love of our Father.

ill know that I am in my Father and you in

FREEDOM

One of the most significant advantages of becoming an adult is that we get to make decisions for ourselves: we take control of our own lives. We are responsible for what we say and do; people show respect to us, and they acknowledge what we do. They treat us like mature people and respect our freedom. If in the past, when things went wrong, we could turn to our parents and withdraw into their safety till things were fixed, now not only do we realise that they cannot change everything to make it better, we do not want them to interfere in the same way because that would be to deny our liberty.

In the same way, God respects our freedom. He acknowledges that we can determine our future and form ourselves. He will not intervene uninvited in our decisions whether they are good or bad, helpful or harmful. God respects our freedom to be who we want to be.

When our life on earth is done, we will see clearly who we have become as a result of our free choices. At the same time, God will look back with us at the truth of who we have become.

At the moment of death we will see our life in a flash; if we are filled with shame it will give rise to fear and fear will turn to hate. If we are ashamed, we will fear God and even hate him because in him we see a truth we cannot accept. Shame causes us to hide from him and not to listen when he calls. This is a lonely place to be: without God and without his love and mercy.

But if when we are at the door of death, we look back over our life and recognise that grace has been its foundation, we will be filled with gratitude and recognise the One who has loved us without limit. Our happiness will be multiplied because we were not blind to that love or to the opportunities that it opened to us. We will finally be with the One who has loved us and our life will become complete in eternal life.

This is why the choices that we make now during our lives are so crucial: this is the reality our freedom is leading to.

Christ freed us to make us *really* free

The more time we spend with people the better we come to know them and the longer it takes for us to say what they are really like. We begin to enjoy the many rich aspects of their personality. Then we feel that we can tell them our story, and listen to theirs.

In the bible we find the stories that people have told about their friendship with God, especially the people who knew Jesus. But we also find the stories of people who struggled to see how God was present with them in their journey through life before Jesus was born and also after he had gone back to the Father.

As they looked at the story of their own lives and read the stories of other people's friendship with God, they came to see a God who was indeed with them in their journey through life, someone who didn't like to interfere with their freedom, but who promised to be with them and to help them – as long as

Hope does not disappoint us because the Holy Spirit has been given to us, pouring into our hearts the love of God. >>>>>>>>>>> Romans chapter five verse five

Faith is the way of holding onto wh

Love always hopes...

>>>>>>>>>> one Corinthians
chapter thirteen verse seven

they were open to his help and love.

It's through reading these stories and then talking to God about what we have read that we come to know him better and come to appreciate just how much of a friend he is to us.

As with any friendship, we also come to understand ourselves a bit better. We begin to see our own story more clearly and realise that our story and God's really do belong together.

We see more and more that our story is a story all about hope.

Hebrews chapter eleven verse one

e hope for, certain of what we cannot see. >>

THE MYSTERY

At the centre of our faith is the Incarnation, the belief that the Son of God took on flesh and became fully human for our sake. The one person, Jesus Christ, is Son of God and Son of Man. He is fully human and fully divine. Although his humanity is complete he is still the Second Person of the Blessed Trinity and as such his divinity is also complete.

God sent his only Son into th

This mystery of Christ is a mystery of love. God decided to reveal the glory of his divinity in the humility of Christ's humanity to teach us that his folly is wiser than our wisdom. All too often we attempt to understand reality. We dissect it and examine its parts to see what it is made from and how it works. We forget to stand in awe at the mystery of what is before us. So in the Incarnation of his Son, God reveals himself in such a way that we can only stand speechless and contemplate the wonder of what he has done.

This is the first and most important lesson of the Incarnation: we are to recapture the wonder of God and of his love for us. For this is what John's letters tell us again and again: to think of the love that the Father has lavished upon us. He tells us that love consists not in our love but in God's love for us when he sent his Son to take away our sins. Our faith is first and foremost about the contemplation and celebration of God's love for us.

By contemplating and celebrating this Mystery we unite our humanity with the gift of divine life given to us by Christ in the sacraments. Our life becomes a celebration – a witness to the Incarnation, to that unity of human and divine which came first in Christ, and is now found in all of us who are baptised.

orld that we might have life through him. >>

THE GOOD NEWS

We all need to be loved and to know that we are loved. It makes such an important difference to our lives if we have that solid basis on which to build for the future.

When Jesus was baptised he came up out of the water to be anointed by the Spirit and Mark tells us that he heard the voice of the Father saying, "You are my Son the beloved, my favour rests on you". We are allowed a glimpse into this very personal moment between God the Father and God the Son. It is a very human moment: the first words of a father to his

My teaching is not mine, but it comes from th

child, an affirmation of acceptance and love. However, it is also the start of the ministry of Jesus when he begins to reveal the Father to us. Everything that Christ says and does from then on is to help us understand that we too are accepted and loved by God.

The measure of God's holiness is his endless love, revealed to us by Christ in everyday human terms. He spoke of God in words of love and hope so that we might understand God and realise that he is not distant from us, but close and caring. He taught about the beauty and sacredness of life given by God as something to be cherished and protected so we will not lose hope, even in the face of suffering and death.

Christ wants us to be filled with hope – a hope that will never be taken from us, even though sometimes the actions of others make it difficult for us to see the beauty of life. The gospels show how trustworthy his word is: when he said someone would be cured they were cured; when he said he would go to someone, he went. His word is truth – utterly dependable. It is God's truth – God's word.

Most of all he shared with us his knowledge about the love of God; once we know about it we will want to share it.

69

ONE THING

Martha, Martha, you worry and are troubled

In the Gospels we hear of the encounters that Jesus had with various people. Those who met him with an open heart were changed when they recognised who he was. People had differing opinions of who he was, but it is Peter's profession of faith in him as the Christ, the Son of God that is exactly right. It is in the faith of Peter and the church that we find a measure of our own encounter with Christ.

When we come before him, then we too must come with an open heart if we are to profit from our encounter with him, whether it is in the sacraments or in our prayer. Only in that openness does our heart recognise him as Christ, the Son of God, and our lips profess him with the same faith as Peter.

In the tradition of the church there have been two well-tried ways of coming to that encounter with Christ. The first is called the *examination of conscience*. It is a simple practice in the evening of taking a few minutes to reflect and become aware of the good things and the bad things in our day. Not only do we look at our actions, we look at the feelings linked with our actions. In this way, we come to recognise the feeling of God's presence

Were not our hearts burning within us while h

with us as well as how it feels when we turn away from him. This is a way of training ourselves to become more aware of God's presence with us and more aware of what is good and what is not good.

The second way of encountering Christ is called *Lectio Divina*. It is a simple way of praying with the bible. Take a passage from the Gospel and read it quietly until you are familiar with the passage. Then take note of what strikes you about what is happening in the passage – you can even write it down, if you wish. Then talk to God about each of the things that you became aware of in the passage. After this you can sit for a while resting in silence.

In these ways we gradually become more aware of Christ and encounter him in our daily life so that we begin to find our life too is changing under his gentle touch.

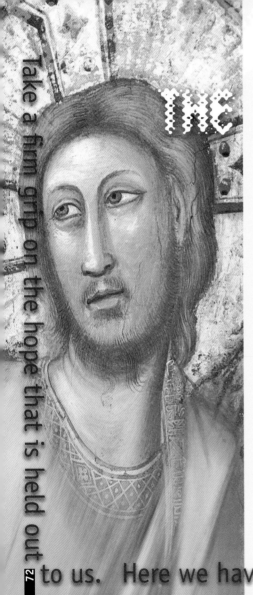

Take a firm grip on the hope that is held out

Do not be afraid...
I am the living one; I wa

THE LIVING ONE

When Christ died on the cross, his disciples were confused and saddened. They had thought that Jesus was going to start a new era in the history of the nation. They had hoped that things would get better for the poor and the oppressed and that they would be able to hold their heads high again. Even though Jesus had tried to teach them that he had to be put to death, they couldn't grasp the bit that he had to die. They didn't understand that the scope of the plan of God the Father was much greater than just making things better for the poor and oppressed. God saw the real oppression we suffer: sin and death.

to us. Here we have an anchor for our soul a

Without the resurrection, the death of Christ would have been like the death of anyone else. If Christ had not risen, it would have meant that evil was stronger than good, death stronger than life, hate more powerful than love; it would have meant that original sin, which brought death into the world, was still undefeated. But because of the resurrection, life has triumphed and in Christ that life is given to all who ask for it.

If we know anything at all about Jesus today it is because of the apostles. The resurrection of Jesus profoundly changed them from fearful fishermen to courageous witnesses. It caused them to rethink their relationship with him and their whole understanding of who God is. They now came to realise that he would be with them always.

It is in the sacraments of baptism and eucharist, when we are made one with Christ, that we come to realise that his risen presence is with us always. In the sacraments we encounter the Living Christ, the Saviour, the bringer of eternal life who sets us free from sin and death.

STAY AWAKE

The Holy Spirit will teach you all things and remind you of all that I have told you. >>>>>

>>>>>> John chapter fourteen verse thirty-six

We all know people who were once full of fun and joy but who changed; we say, 'the life has gone out of them'. We don't mean that they have died, we just mean that there is something missing, the spark that was once there has gone from them.

When Jesus was speaking of the Holy Spirit he spoke of the life of God. The Spirit is that divine spark, the breath of God that passes between the Father and Son, the love of God that unites Son and Father. When he died on the cross, Christ breathed out that Spirit to share it with us. From that moment on we could share in this divine life. With the death of Christ the Spirit was sent out to be given on Easter

Jesus said to them, "Peac

Sunday. This is what we celebrate at Pentecost and it is this same Spirit we receive at confirmation.

Christ calls the Spirit the Advocate because the Spirit prays with us and on our behalf. We all know at times the power of sin. Out of the blue we do things which are not in keeping with our ideals and, as soon as we have done them, we regret them. We also know the power of the Spirit in us when we are kind, when we find the right words to help someone, or when we find the strength to do what is right, then we are just as sure it is a grace given us by the Spirit.

It is the Spirit in us that helps us grow in our knowledge of God and of God's love for us. It is the Spirit who encourages us to cry out to God as Father. It is the Spirit who brings alive what we say in our prayer and profess in our faith. The Spirit is the greatest gift that Christ has to give to us, because it is a share in the very life of God.

e with you. As the Father has sent me

so I send you."….he breathed on them and said to them, "Receive the Holy Spirit."

>>>>>>>>>>>>>>>> John chapter twenty verse twenty-one

THE PROMISE

Just as a family is a group of people related by blood and by love, so the Church thinks of itself as a group of people related by the blood of Christ and by our love for each other – God's family. That is what baptism is about.

When Jesus gathered a group of twelve around him they got to know him and told others about him. At first they thought he was a prophet or maybe even the promised messiah, but it was only after the resurrection and the coming of the Spirit that they began to understand the full truth of who he was. They came to a new understanding of everything he had said and done before he was crucified. As time passed the Church became this group of people who came together to listen to the good news about Jesus and to reflect on it, so that they would get a better understanding of God as Jesus revealed him.

The kingdom of God is among you. >>>>>

A great crowd, impossible to count, from every nation, race, people and tongue... >>>>>>
>>>>>> Revelation chapter seven verse nine

He taught them many things through stories or parables. >>>>>>>>>>>>>>>>>>>>>>>

This people still comes together to share the story of Christ and to share their own stories and as they do they realise that it is really just one big story. As with every story, the truth becomes clearer the longer we continue with the story. We call this truth that is emerging, *tradition* – something that we hand on to each generation.

But not everyone has Christ in their story so our story as Christians is different from that of others. Perhaps this difference is seen most clearly in Christ's promise of eternal life to his followers, and so our story is about waiting for him to come and fulfil that promise.

But it isn't just about waiting. Because of his resurrection Christ is our contemporary. Through our relationship with him we are transformed. So as we wait with hope and confidence, we live freely in faith and share with others the joy that this faith brings.

IN HER HEART

Speed is of the essence, not because we can get home sooner or can get things done quicker and have more time to ourselves, but because it stops us becoming impatient with waiting.

We live in a time where immediacy is demanded: we want everything yesterday if at all possible, but it doesn't seem to give us any more time, or make our life any better, because there is always something else for us to do. When we think we are going to have to spend time waiting, we fill it up with noise or pictures or whatever is available to us. Increasingly we close ourselves off to what is going on around us and withdraw into our own little cocoon.

The Gospels don't say much about Mary, the mother of Jesus, but one thing they do say about her is that she watched what was going on and pondered it in her heart. She stopped and enjoyed what was going on around her, not only to enjoy it but to contemplate it. She did this especially with her son: with his life and his teaching.

In our world the danger is that we are too rushed off our feet, too isolated from our surroundings to be able to appreciate what we see, to

She kept all these things in her heart. >>

wonder at it and to enjoy it. If we never give ourselves time to really look at what we see and to drink in its beauty, then we will never be able to stand in awe before it. We will never hear it speak to us of the beauty of God and we will think that God is far from us.

Mary took time in silence to be there with Christ and to attend to what he was doing and saying. She took time to be there with creation around her so that the beauty she saw outside became one with the beauty that was within her. She was able to recognise the beauty of God when the time came for her to see it in all its glory. What a joy life is when we give ourselves the time to feel that beauty of creation and of Christ around and within us.

>>>>>>>>> Luke chapter two verse fifty-one

As for Mary, she treasured all these messages and continually pondered over them. ^^^^^^^^^^^
^ Luke chapter two verse nineteen

LOVE

We come alive

when we are with others because we are made in the image and likeness of the Trinity. They are one in their relationship with one another: Father, Son and Spirit. And so if we are to understand ourselves, it must be in relationship with others. We feel ourselves to be the most complete not when we are alone, but when we are with others.

It was Christ who told us that God is love. God is this

perfect giving of the Father to the Son and the Son to the Father, so perfect that the giving is the Holy Spirit. Our perfection comes in the giving of ourselves in love to another because we share in this life of God. The more we give of ourselves in this way, the more that life is alive in us, and consequently the more we live the divine life given to us in baptism and confirmation and then nurtured in the eucharist.

It is only in living this life of loving charity that we come to understand the triune God, not from the outside but from within because we share in the very life of God. The knowledge we have of God is not that of an external observer, but of one who shares in the intimacy of their life.

It is the persons of the Trinity who give birth to all life and who draw all life back to themselves. We can either struggle against that, as we do when we sin, and deny our very nature as an image of that love, or we can be part of that stream of life-giving love. That is why Christ said there are two commandments: love of God and love of neighbour.

God and the fellowship of the Holy Spirit be with you all. >>>>>>>>>>>>>>>>>>>>>>>> two Corinthians chapter thirteen verse thirteen

race of Christ Jesus the Lord, the love of

Life is a gift
with many opportunities.

Each moment is unique,
unrepeatable.

This moment will only happen once!

When moments are past
we are left with the memories.

Memories are precious,
and as you survive
the rest of your life,
your memories become more precious.

Invite those people
who have had an impact on your life
so far to sign a message
on the pages that follow...

Keep your memories for life.

THOUGHTS

AND MEMORIES

MEMORIES

The only real aging process is
the erosion of our ideals. Albert Schweitzer

Celebrate what you want to see more of! Thomas Peters

All — everything I understand,
I understand
only because I love.
Leo Tolstoy

The only people who never fail are those who never try.

Ilka Chase

We live forward

Søren Kierkegaard

Hope is not the conviction that something will turn out well but the certainty that something makes sense regardless of how it turns out.

Václav Havel

SOME COOL WEB SITES 4 U

http://www.life4seekers.co.uk

to improve life and find a new sense of fulfilment, fresh energy and the joy of living //// with lots of quotes, comments, viewpoints... and more!

http://www.godspy.com

a vibrant on-line magazine for Catholics and other seekers //// explores ideas and experiences that reveal God's presence in the world: from politics to the arts, science to economy, sexuality to ecology...

http://www.disciplesnow.com

an informational resource //// opportunities to learn, to discuss and to celebrate the challenges of discipleship in the context of daily life

http://www.lifeteen.org

resources and training to encourage vibrant Eucharistic celebrations plus opportunities for faith development

http://www.catholicireland.net

sections include spirituality, faith and justice, youth focus, culture, the arts and more...

http://www.sacredspace.ie

ten minute daily scriptural prayer – on-line!